The Famous Five

Terry Barber

ACTIVIST SERIES

The Famous Five is published by
Grass Roots Press, a division of Literacy Services of Canada Ltd.

PHONE 1–888–303–3213
WEBSITE www.literacyservices.com

ACKNOWLEDGEMENTS

We would like to thank the Famous 5 Foundation for reviewing the manuscript. For more information, visit their website at www.famous5.org.

We acknowledge the financial support of the Government of Canada through the Book Publishing Industry Development Program (BPIDP) for our publishing activities.

We acknowledge the support of the Alberta Foundation for the Arts for our publishing programs.

Editor: Dr. Pat Campbell
Image Research: Dr. Pat Campbell
Book design: Lara Minja, Lime Design Inc.

Library and Archives Canada Cataloguing in Publication

Barber, Terry, date
    The Famous Five / Terry Barber.

(Activist series)
ISBN 1–894593–52–9

    1. Readers for new literates. 2. Famous Five (Canadian women's rights activists) I. Title. II. Series.

HQ1455.A3B37 2006   428.6'2   C2006–903728–0

Printed in Canada

Contents

The Famous Five meet for tea.

Five Women Meet for Tea

Emily Murphy invites four women to her home. Emily wants these women to help her. Emily wants to change the laws of the land. These women will become known as The Famous Five.

The Famous Five live in Alberta, Canada.

The Early 1900s

It is the early 1900s. Women do not have basic rights. They cannot vote. They cannot own property. They cannot serve in the Senate. The law does not give women the same rights as men.

A mother reads to her child, 1900.

The Early 1900s

Many men think their wives should stay at home. Women should raise the children. Women should do as they are told. By men, of course. Women need to know their place. And their place is in the home.

A woman washes clothes, 1905.

These women clean and press clothes, 1909.

The Early 1900s

Some women work outside the home.
Men get the good jobs. Women get
the **dead-end jobs.** Sometimes, men
and women work at the same job.
But women get paid less than men.

This woman makes butter in the farm house.

The Early 1900s

Many families live on farms. The farm wives work very hard. They work in the house. They work in the fields. Farm wives work as hard as their husbands. But, the law says women cannot own the farm.

This woman cuts oats in the fields, 1909.

The men go to war.

The Early 1900s

In 1914, many men go to war. Many women are left at home. Women must fill the men's jobs. Women show they are strong. Women show they are smart. But they still do not have the same rights as men.

World War I lasts from 1914 to 1918. Over 600,000 Canadian men fight in the war.

A woman works in a factory, 1917.

Henrietta Muir
Edwards

Louise McKinney

Irene Parlby

Emily Murphy

Nellie McClung

The Famous Five

Five women decide to make life better for women and children. Their names are Emily Murphy, Nellie McClung, Louise McKinney, Henrietta Muir Edwards, and Irene Parlby. They believe women should have the same rights as men.

Emily Murphy, 1919.

The Famous Five

Emily Murphy is Canada's first female judge. She fights for laws that protect women and children. She is also a writer. Emily writes about the drug trade. Her writing results in new laws about drugs.

Nellie McClung

The Famous Five

Nellie McClung is a famous writer. She gives speeches about women's rights. She knows how to put words into action. She fights for the rights of women in Canada.

Nellie McClung and her son, 1910.

Louise McKinney, 1917.

The Famous Five

Louise McKinney is a Christian. She helps form the United Church of Canada. She believes people should not drink. She fights for stronger liquor laws.

In 1917, Louise McKinney is the first woman elected to Canada's government.

Henrietta Muir Edwards

The Famous Five

Henrietta Muir Edwards starts a magazine. It is Canada's first magazine for women. It is called *Working Women of Canada*. Henrietta knows about laws that affect women. She knows how to change these laws.

Irene Parlby, 1928.

The Famous Five

Irene Parlby supports farm women. She is president of the United Farm Women of Alberta. She believes in better education for women. She believes in better health care for women. She believes women should get better pay.

Irene Parlby is the first female **cabinet minister** in Alberta.

This woman does not have property rights.

Property Rights

Women do not have property rights. If a husband divorces his wife, he gets the property. If a husband dies, the woman does not get the property. This is the law. The property rights law does not protect women.

The Dower Act is passed in the
Alberta Legislature.

Property Rights

The Famous Five work to change this law. The **Dower Act** is passed in 1911. This law gives a woman the right to one-third of her husband's property.

Voting Rights

In 1915 women cannot vote. The Famous Five are leaders in the voting rights movement. They give speeches. They plan a sit-in. They force the government to change the law.

These women vote for the first time.

Voting Rights

By 1916, women can vote in three provinces. Quebec is the last province to give women the right to vote. Quebec women cannot vote until 1940.

In 1918, women also win the right to vote in federal elections.

The Person's Case

Emily Murphy wants to become Canada's first female **senator.** In the eyes of the law, a woman is not a person. This means that women cannot serve in the Senate.

Emily Murphy works as a judge, 1917.

The Person's Case

Murphy wants to change the federal law. She asks her friends to help her. In 1917, the Famous Five work together to change the law. It takes a long time.

Women become persons on October 18, 1929.

The Person's Case

In 1929, the law is changed. The new law says that women are "persons." Now, women can serve in Canada's Senate.

There is a sad note to this story. Emily Murphy does not become a senator. She dies in 1933.

Emily Murphy's funeral.

The sky is now her limit.

Pushing for Change

The Famous Five fought for women's rights. They help to change laws. Women win the right to vote. Women gain property rights. And women can serve in the Senate.

Emily Murphy, 1926.

Pushing for Change

Emily Murphy liked to say: "Nothing happens by chance. Everything is pushed from behind." Emily knew how to push. The Famous Five knew how to push. They pushed Canada to change its laws.

Glossary

cabinet minister: an elected member of the government. A cabinet minister usually manages a government department.

dead-end job: a job that does not promote a person's skills.

Dower Act: a law that allows a woman legal rights to her husband's property.

senator: In Canada, these people are appointed by the Governor General. They make decisions about legislation.

Talking About the Book

What did you learn about The Famous Five?

How did society treat women in the early 1900s?

Do you think women have equal rights in today's society?

Emily Murphy used to say: "Nothing happens by chance. Everything is pushed from behind." What do you think this means?

How did the Famous Five make the world a better place?

Picture Credits

Front cover photos (center photo): (c) Library of Congress, Prints and Photographs Division, LC-USZ62-75334 DLC; **(small photo):** (c) Helen Siemens. **Contents page (top):** Library of Congress, Prints and Photographs Division, LC-DIG-nclc-04244; **(bottom):** © Library of Congress, Prints and Photographs Division, LC-USZ62-23622 DLC. **Page 4:** © Helen Siemens. **Page 6:** © Library of Congress, Prints and Photographs Division, LC-USZC2-1088. **Page 8:** © Glenbow Archives NC-39-321. **Page 9:** © Library of Congress, Prints and Photographs Division, LC-USZ62-102221. **Page 10:** © Library and Archives Canada/PA 96079. **Page 12:** © Glenbow Archives NA-2133-2. **Page 13:** © Glenbow Archives NC-43-13. **Page 14:** © City of Edmonton Archives EA-10-795. **Page 15:** © Library and Archives Canada/PA 24640. **Page 16 (top row left):** Glenbow Archives NA-2607-7; **(top row middle):** Glenbow Archives NA-1731-3; **(top row right):** NA-273-1; **(bottom row left):** City of Edmonton Archives EA-10-1987; **(bottom row right):** Glenbow Archives NA-273-2. **Page 18:** © City of Edmonton Archives EA-10-2026. **Page 20:** © Glenbow Archives NA-1641-1. **Page 21:** © Library and Archives Canada/C-008482. **Page 22:** © Glenbow Archives NA-5395-4. **Page 24:** © Glenbow Archives NA-4035-138. **Page 26:** © Glenbow Archives NA-2204-12. **Page 27:** © Glenbow Archives NA-142-2. **Page 28:** © Library of Congress, Prints and Photographs Division, LC-USZ62-123545. **Page 32:** © Library of Congress, Prints and Photographs Division, LC-USZ62-23622 DLC. **Page 34:** © Library of Congress, Prints and Photographs Division, LC-USZ62-75334 DLC. **Page 36:** © Library of Congress, Prints and Photographs Division, LC-USZC4-2905. **Page 38:** © Glenbow Archives NC-6-2906. **Page 40:** © Helen Siemens. **Page 41:** © Glenbow Archives ND-3-6518a. **Page 42:** © Library of Congress, Prints and Photographs Division, LC-DIG-ppmsca-02919. **Page 44:** © City of Edmonton Archives EA-10-1979.